# Andrew Brodie Basics
# LET'S DO GRAMMAR

## FOR AGES 5-6

- Over 50 activities
- Regular progress tests
- Matched to the National Curriculum

with over **100** reward stickers

Andrew Brodie
An imprint of Bloomsbury Publishing Plc

50 Bedford Square
London
WC1B 3DP
UK

1385 Broadway
New York
NY 10018
USA

**www.bloomsbury.com**

ANDREW BRODIE is a trademark of Bloomsbury Publishing Plc

First published in Great Britain 2017

ISBN
PB: 978-1-4729-4060-5
ePDF: 978-1-4729-4059-9

2 4 6 8 10 9 7 5 3 1

Designed and typeset by Marcus Duck Design
Printed and bound in China by Leo Paper Products

To find out more about our authors and books visit www.bloomsbury.com.
Here you will find extracts, author interviews, details of forthcoming events and the
option to sign up for our newsletters.

## BLOOMSBURY

# Notes for parents

## What's in this book

This is the first in the series of *Andrew Brodie Basics: Let's Do Grammar* books. Each book features a clearly structured approach to developing and improving children's knowledge and use of grammar in their reading and writing as well as in their oral communication.

The National Curriculum states that children in Year 1 should learn appropriate terminology in relation to grammar and punctuation, including the following:

- letter, capital letter
- word, singular, plural
- sentence
- punctuation, full stop, question mark, exclamation mark.

Children will learn to create sentences, leaving appropriate spaces between words, and will learn to punctuate their sentences with a capital letter at the start and a full stop, question mark or exclamation mark at the end. They will join words and join clauses using the word 'and'. They will use capital letters for names of people, places, the days of the week and the personal pronoun 'I'.

To improve their grammatical vocabulary, children will be introduced to suffixes that can be added to singular nouns to make them plural. They will also learn about suffixes such as *ing*, *ed* and *er* that can change verbs, e.g. *play* becoming *playing*, *played* and *player*, as well as the prefix *un* changing words such as *happy* to *unhappy*.

## How you can help

Make sure your child is ready for their grammar practice and help them to enjoy it using the activities in this book. If necessary, read through each activity out loud, discussing it so that your child really understands what the writing means.

The answer section at the end of this book can be a useful teaching tool: ask your child to compare their responses to the ones shown. Their answers may not be identical but should include similar information. If your child has made mistakes, help them to learn from them. Remember that the speed at which your child progresses will vary from topic to topic.

Most importantly, enjoy the experience of working with your child and sharing the excitement of learning together.

## Look out for...

**Pedro the Panda**, who will help your child understand what to focus on when working through the activities.

**Brodie's Brain Boosters**, which feature quick extra activities designed to make your child think, using the skills and knowledge they already have. Can they talk about their experiences using appropriate and interesting vocabulary?

# Contents

# Criss-cross

**Read the words below.**

big   kind   ~~sad~~   cold   mean   ~~happy~~

little   easy   hard   far   near   hot

**Write the words in the criss-cross boxes. Each criss-cross should contain a pair of opposite words. One has been done for you.**

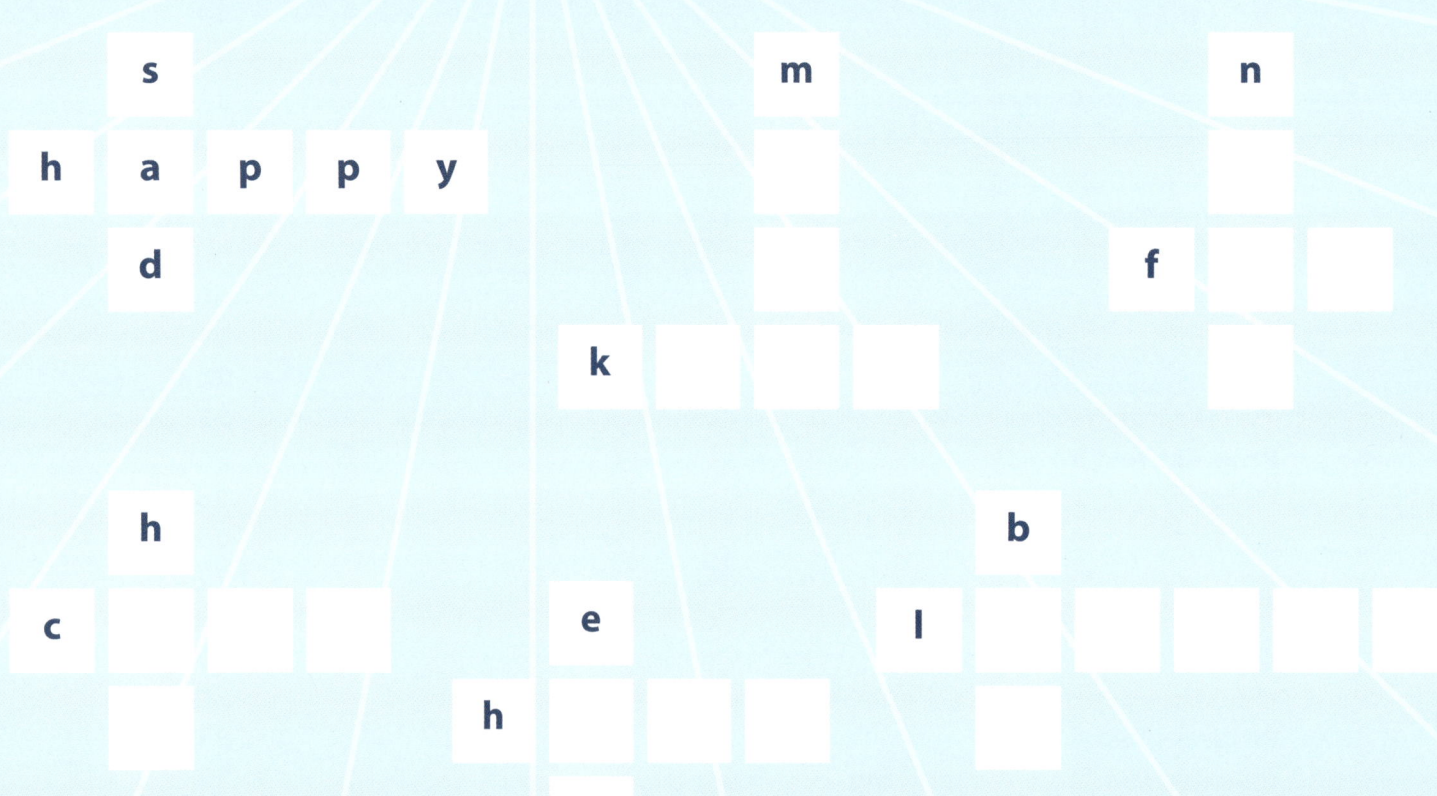

```
        s                    m                        n
h   a   p   p   y

        d                                        f  □  □

                    k  □  □  □  □                    □


        h                                    b
c   □   □   □               e            l   □   □   □   □   □   □
        □               h   □   □            □
                        □
                        □
```

## Brodie's Brain Booster

Can you think of a word that means the opposite of **up**?

# More opposites

Some opposites can be made by adding **un** to the start of the word..

Write the missing words in the chart.
The first one has been done for you.

| Word | Opposite |
|---|---|
| happy | unhappy |
| kind |  |
| afraid |  |
|  | unzip |
| block |  |
|  | uncover |
| fit |  |
|  | unhook |
| join |  |
| lock |  |
|  | unpack |
| tie |  |
| safe |  |

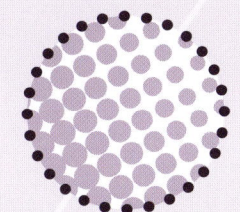

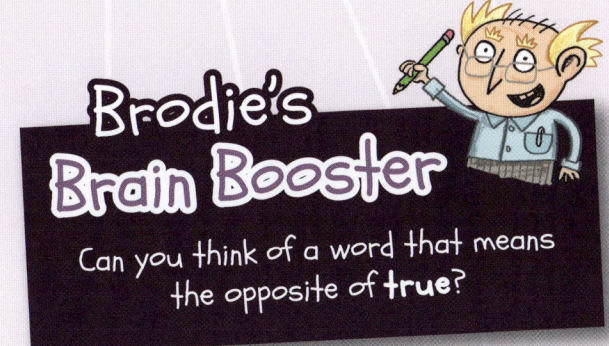

Brodie's
**Brain Booster**
Can you think of a word that means
the opposite of **true**?

 # Odd one out

Look carefully at all the words in each line.

**Can you find the odd one out in each line?
The first one has been done for you.**

| happy | merry | jolly | (unhappy) |
| small | big | huge | gigantic |
| kind | unkind | friendly | nice |
| unpack | load | fill | pack |
| thin | thick | narrow | small |
| afraid | scared | frightened | unafraid |
| hot | warm | cold | boiling |

## Brodie's Brain Booster

Can you think of a word that means nearly the same as **tall**?

# Happy and unhappy

Don't forget the full stop at the end of each sentence.

**Read the words below.**

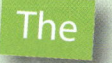 The  has a 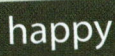 has happy is boy is arm

 hurt girl The cake He She her unhappy

**Use these words to write two sentences for each picture. Don't forget the full stops.**

_____

_____

_____

_____

_____

_____

_____

_____

## Brodie's Brain Booster

What makes you happy? Make up a sentence about it.

7

# A happy picture

Can you think of any other words that mean **happy**?

Draw a happy picture. Who is in the picture? It could be you. It could be your mum. It could be anybody. You can choose.

Now write a sentence about your happy picture.

_____

_____

_____

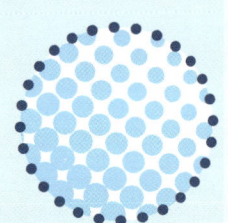

Brodie's
Brain Booster

Who can you make happy?
Make up a sentence about it.

# Opposite directions

Remember, each sentence must start with a capital letter.

**Look at the pictures. Can you tell the story?
Don't forget to write in sentences.**

_____

_____

_____

_____

_____

_____

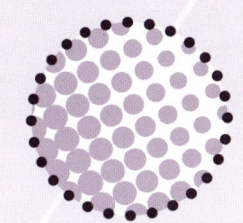

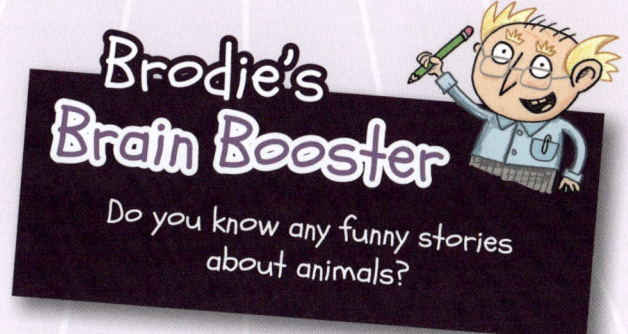

Brodie's
Brain Booster

Do you know any funny stories
about animals?

**Write the opposite of each of these words.**

up _____ wet _____

hot _____ tall _____

sad _____ high _____

**Write the opposite of each of these words.**

able _____ unkind _____

zip _____ unlock _____

wrap _____ unwise _____

**Can you find the odd one out in each line?
The first one has been done for you.**

uneven          unblock          (clean)          unsure
_____

tall          small          big          huge
_____

damp          soaking          wet          dry

**Write a sentence about the picture.**

_____

_____

_____

# One or more

Do you know what **singular** means?

**one cat**

**three cats**

The word **cat** is a singular word.

The word **cats** is a plural word.

## Change these singular words to plural words.

dog _____     chair _____

boy _____     clock _____

girl _____     book _____

house _____     eye _____

tree _____     ear _____

car _____     nose _____

table _____     mouth _____

### Brodie's Brain Booster

The word **mouse** is a singular word. Do you know what the plural is?

# More than one

one fox

three foxes

The word **fox** is a
singular word.

The word **foxes** is a
plural word.

Did you notice that **es** was added to the singular word to make it plural?
Change these singular words to plural words.

potato _____     match _____

tomato _____     bush _____

church _____     echo _____

ditch _____     wish _____

switch _____     kiss _____

dish _____     bus _____

splash _____     hero _____

## Brodie's Brain Booster

The word **child** is a singular word.
Can you change it to a plural word?

12

# Find the plural words

Can you find all the plural words?

Look for the plural words.

They may be written across, like this: c a t s

They may be written down, like this: 
d
o
g
s

| a | b | t | a | b | l | e | s | c | d |
| e | f | g | h | o | i | j | k | l | d |
| m | n | o | c | o | w | s | p | q | i |
| r | s | t | u | k | v | o | w | x | s |
| b | o | x | e | s | y | c | z | a | h |
| b | c | d | e | f | g | k | h | i | e |
| j | k | s | p | l | a | s | h | e | s |
| l | m | n | o | p | q | r | s | t | u |
| v | w | x | t | r | e | e | s | y | z |
| p | i | n | s | a | b | c | d | e | f |

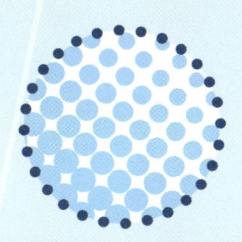

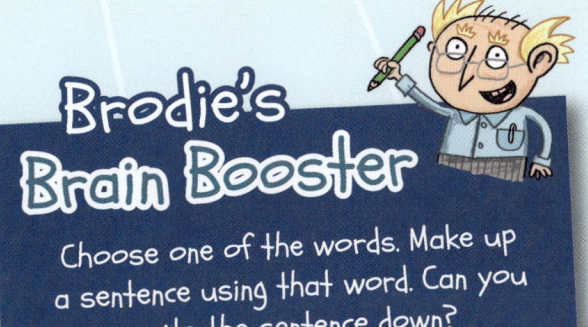

## Brodie's Brain Booster

Choose one of the words. Make up a sentence using that word. Can you write the sentence down?

13

# Special plural words

**one mouse**

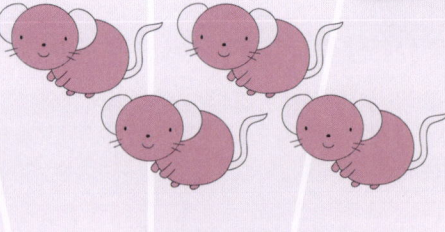

**four mice**

The word **mouse** is a singular word.

The word **mice** is a plural word.

**Read the words below.**

children    mice    women    men    ladies    babies    tooth

**Change these singular words to plural words.**

baby _____    lady _____

mouse _____    woman _____

child _____    man _____

**Write a sentence about this picture.**

_____

_____

_____

**Brodie's Brain Booster**

The word **goose** is a singular word. Do you know what the plural is?

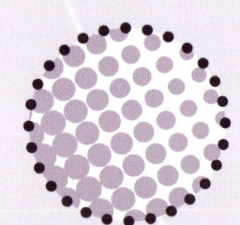

14

# Odd one out

Look carefully at all the words in each line.

Can you find the **odd one out** in each line?
The first one has been done for you.

| | | | |
|---|---|---|---|
| flower | plant | (trees) | shrub |
| car | bus | motorbike | lorries |
| baby | boy | children | girl |
| girls | babies | boys | child |
| houses | flat | bungalow | house |
| bricks | tiles | brick | blocks |
| flower | leaf | petal | leaves |

**Brodie's Brain Booster**

Do you know the plural word for **deer**?

# Criss-cross

**Read the words below.**

~~child~~   deer   geese   teeth   babies   baby

tooth   goose   deer   ~~children~~   match   matches

**Write the words in the criss-cross boxes. Each criss-cross should contain a singular word and a plural word to go with it. One has been done for you.**

**Brodie's Brain Booster**

What is the plural of **foot**?

16

**Change these plural words to singular words.**

girls _____     rabbits _____

boys _____      cars _____

matches _____   buses _____

foxes _____     coaches _____

dishes _____    houses _____

**Change these plural words to singular words.**

mice _____      women _____

children _____  deer _____

ponies _____    teeth _____

ladies _____    geese _____

men _____       lorries _____

**Choose three of the plural words above. Write a sentence for each word.**

_____

_____

_____

_____

_____

_____

# Capital letters

Look at the pictures and write a story to go with them. Don't forget to write in sentences. Remember, each sentence must start with a capital letter.

_____

_____

_____

_____

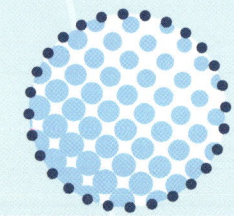

**What happened next?**

_____

_____

_____

_____

**Brodie's Brain Booster**

What do you think will happen next?

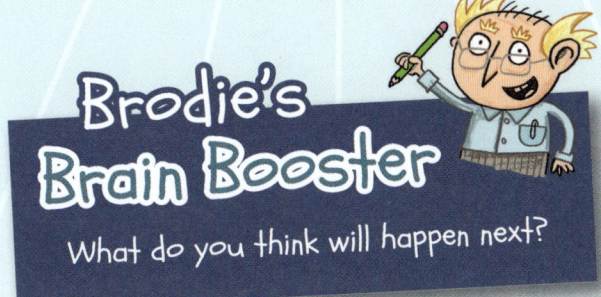

19

# Names

Every name should start with a capital letter.

Someone has written these names wrongly. They have forgotten to use a capital letter at the start of each name. Write them again properly. The first one has been done for you.

ava _____Ava_____

gabriel _____

benjamin _____

holly _____

connor _____

isaac _____

daisy _____

james _____

elliot _____

katie _____

faith _____

letisha _____

## Brodie's Brain Booster

Do you know the name of all the children your class?

# Alphabetical order

Remember that every name needs to start with a capital letter.

Here is the alphabet in lower case letters.

a b c d e f g h i j k l m n o p q r s t u v w x y z

Here is the alphabet in capital letters.

A B C D E F G H I J K L M N O P Q R S T U V W X Y Z

Read the names then write them in alphabetical order.

Ali   Jude   Willow   Harvey   Poppy   Muhammad   Isla   Tommy   Yara

Liam   Xavier   Dylan   Ruby   Grace   Felix   Blake   Clara   Omar

Eliza   Katie   Umar   Nur   Zoe   Violet   Seth   Queenie

Ali

Blake

Clara

Brodie's
Brain Booster

Can you think of any other name beginning with Z?

# Days of the week

Every day of the week should start with a capital letter.

Monday    Friday    Sunday    Tuesday

Wednesday    Saturday    Thursday

**Write the days of the week in order. The first one has been done for you.**

_Monday_

_____    _____

_____    _____

_____    _____

_____

**What day comes after Thursday?** _____

**What day comes just before Sunday?** _____

**What day comes after Tuesday?** _____

**What day comes just before Monday?** _____

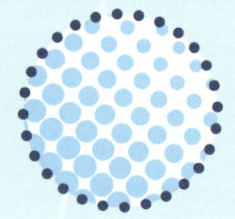

Brodie's Brain Booster

What is your favourite day of the week? Why is it your favourite?

22

# My favourite day

**Which is your favourite day of the week?**

_____

**Draw a picture about your favourite day of the week.**

**Write about your favourite day of the week.**

_____

_____

_____

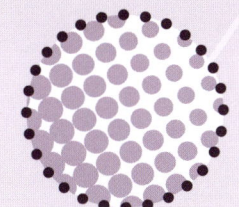

Brodie's Brain Booster

Which two days are at the weekend?

23

**Write the full names of four people in your family.**

_____

_____

_____

_____

**Write the days of the week in order.**

_____

_____

_____

_____

_____

_____

_____

**Write two sentences about what you do at the weekend.**

_____

_____

_____

_____

# London

These are some famous places in London.

Buckingham Palace

The Tower of London

Tower Bridge

Wembley Stadium

Names of places always start with a capital letter.

Write the correct name next to each picture.
Don't forget to start each name with a capital letter.

_____

_____

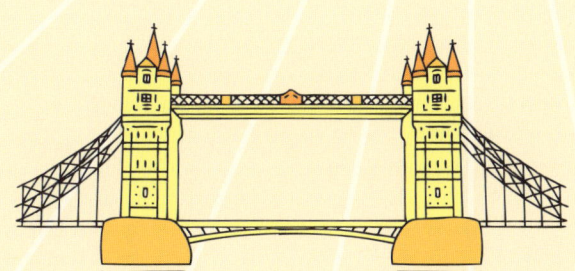

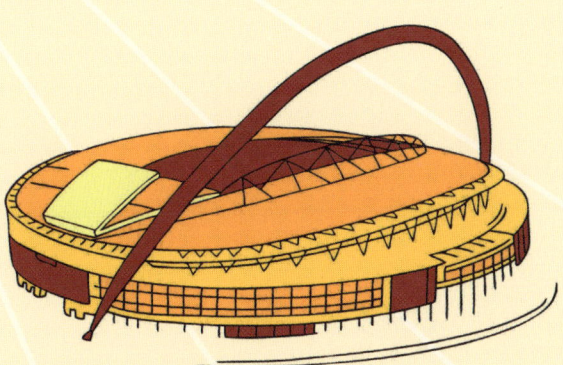

_____

_____

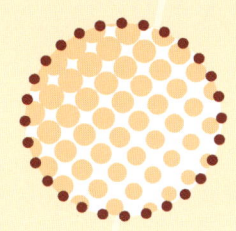

Brodie's Brain Booster

Have you ever been to London?

25

# My address

I live in China.

Look at Tom's address.

17 Bradford Road     This is Tom's house number.

Tolwater     This is his road.

Somerset     This is the town where Tom lives.

TA9 7DY     This is the county.

This is the postcode.

Write your name and address on this envelope.
You might need some help.

_____

_____

_____

_____

_____

## Brodie's Brain Booster

How many towns can you name?

# A place I have visited

I have been to lots of places.

**Draw a picture of a place you have visited.**

**Write some sentences about the place you have drawn. Don't forget to use a capital letter for the start of each name.**

_____

_____

_____

_____

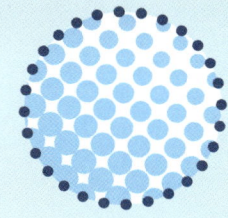

Brodie's
Brain Booster

Where is your favourite place?

# Questions and answers

You should always use a question mark at the end of a question.

This is a question mark. **?**

Here are some question sentences. Each one ends with a question mark.

What is your full name?
How old are you?
How many people are in your family?
Where do you live?

Write the answers to the questions.

_____

_____

_____

_____

_____

_____

Brodie's Brain Booster

Can you think of some questions?

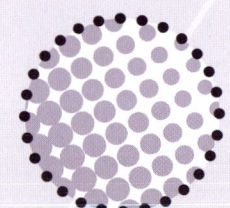

# Writing questions

**Write the question mark carefully.**

**Start here** →  **Write the dot last**

**Write five questions to ask someone. Make sure each one ends with a question mark.**

1. _____

2. _____

3. _____

4. _____

5. _____

**Brodie's Brain Booster**

Do you know what an exclamation mark is?

# Questions about places

Don't forget that place names start with capital letters.

**Write a sentence to answer each question.**

**What is the name of your home town?**

_____

**What is the name of your school?**

_____

**Draw a picture of you on holiday.**

**Where did you go on holiday?**

_____

### Brodie's Brain Booster

Do you know where this famous tower is?

Someone has written these place names wrongly. They have forgotten to use a capital letter at the start of each place name. Write them again properly.

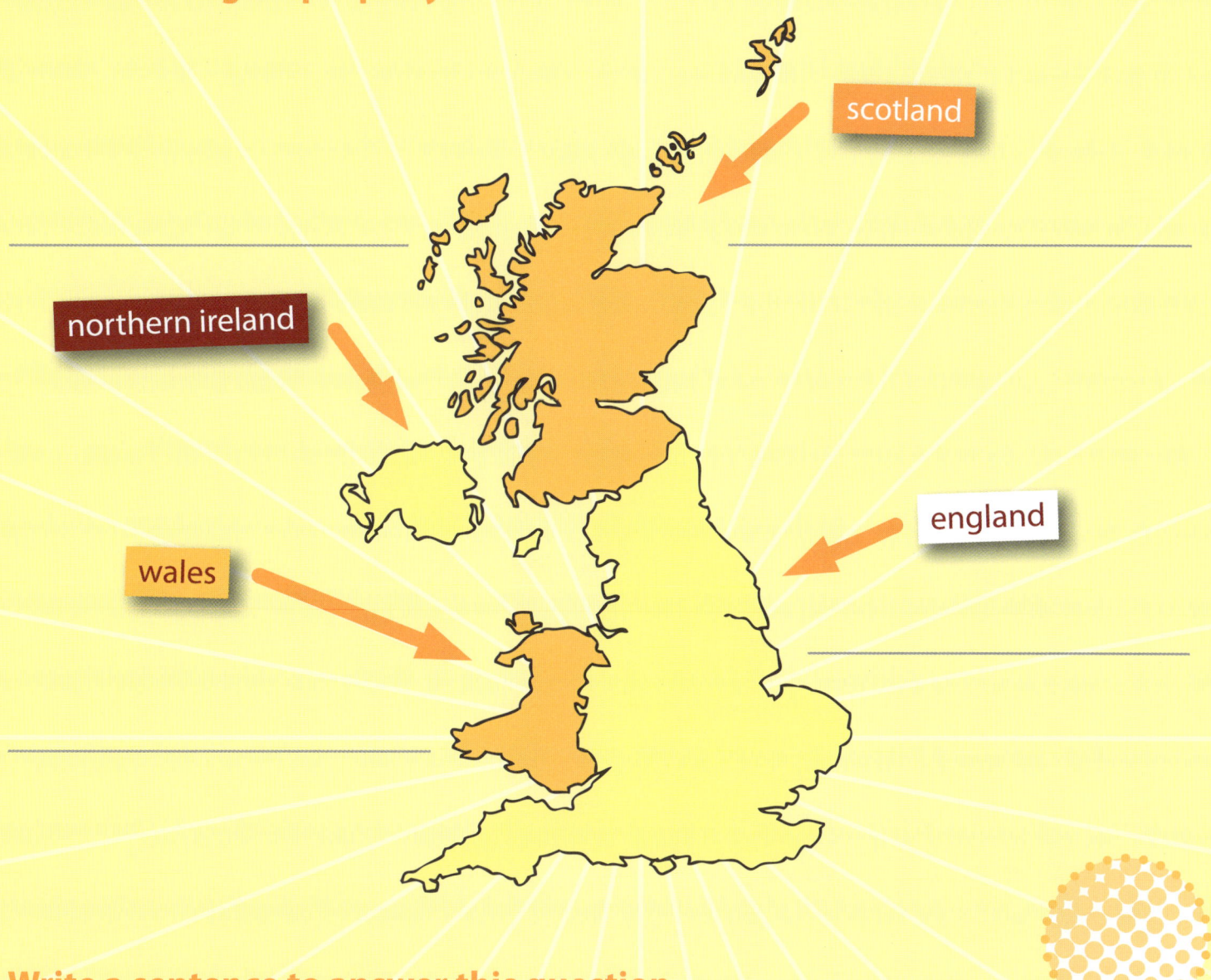

scotland

northern ireland

england

wales

_____

_____

_____

_____

Write a sentence to answer this question.
What country do you live in?

_____

Write a question about a place. Ask someone to answer your question.

_____

_____

# Changing words by adding ing

I like eating bamboo.

Look at the word eat.

# eat

Look at the word eating.

# eating

Change the following words by adding **ing** to each one.

play _____  sing _____

jump _____  act _____

build _____  draw _____

park _____  read _____

Draw a picture that shows one of the **ing** words. Write some sentences about your picture.

_____

_____

_____

_____

_____

_____

_____

Brodie's Brain Booster

What do you like eating?

# Find the ing words

**Look for the ing words.**

**They may be written across, like this:** ending

**They may be written down, like this:** dusting

**There are seven words to find. One has been done for you.**

| a | b | t | a | b | l | e | s | c | d |
|---|---|---|---|---|---|---|---|---|---|
| e | f | g | h | a | s | k | i | n | g |
| m | c | o | c | r | w | s | n | q | a |
| r | r | t | u | k | v | o | g | x | r |
| b | o | x | e | i | y | c | i | a | d |
| b | s | d | e | n | g | k | n | i | e |
| j | s | i | n | g | i | n | g | e | n |
| l | i | n | o | p | q | r | s | t | i |
| s | n | o | w | i | n | g | s | y | n |
| p | g | n | s | a | b | c | d | e | g |

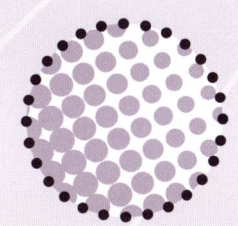

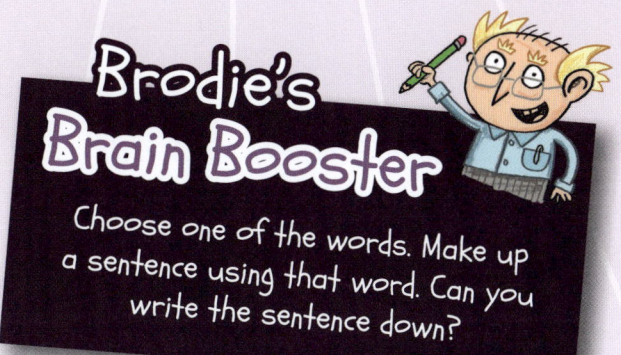

Brodie's Brain Booster

Choose one of the words. Make up a sentence using that word. Can you write the sentence down?

33

# Adding ed to words

I like to paint. I painted a picture.

**Look at the word paint.**

# paint

**Look at the word painted.**

# painted

**Change these words by adding ed to each one.**

jump _____    act _____

look _____    join _____

bark _____    watch _____

play _____    peck _____

**Draw a picture that shows one of the ed words. Write some sentences about your picture.**

_____

_____

_____

_____

_____

_____

Brodie's
Brain Booster

Talk about a picture you have painted.

# Criss-cross

All the words are about sounds.

**Read the words below.**

~~scream~~    barked    yelled    shouted    roar    roared

~~screamed~~    shout    whispered    yell    whisper    bark

**Write the words in the criss-cross boxes. Each criss-cross should contain a pair of sound words. One has been done for you.**

```
        s                           s
        c                           c
        r                   s _ _ _ _ _ _
s c r e a m e d                     _
        a                           _
        m
                            b
        w               b _ _ _ _ _
        _                 _
w _ _ _ _ _ _ _ _ _       _       y
        _                 _       _
        _             y _ _ _ _ _ _
        _         r       _       _
        _     r _ _ _
                  _
                  _
                  _
```

**Brodie's Brain Booster**

Can you think of any other sound words?

35

# Adding er to words

I like to play football.
I am a football player.

Look at the word play.

# play

Look at the word player.

# player

Change the following words by adding **er** to each one.

jump _____    hunt _____

dance _____    buzz _____

quick _____    send _____

fresh _____    sing _____

Draw a picture that shows one of the **ed** words. Write some sentences about your picture.

_____

_____

_____

_____

_____

_____

**Brodie's Brain Booster**

Are you a dancer, a player, a jumper or a singer?

# Find the er words

Can you find all the words ending with **er**?

Look for the **er** words.

They may be written **across**, like this:  watcher

They may be written **down**, like this:
r
i
n
g
e
r

**There are eight words to find. One has been done for you.**

| a | b | w | a | t | c | h | e | r | d |
|---|---|---|---|---|---|---|---|---|---|
| e | f | a | h | a | s | k | i | i | g |
| m | i | l | l | e | r | s | n | n | a |
| r | r | k | u | k | e | o | g | g | r |
| b | o | e | e | i | a | c | i | e | d |
| b | s | r | e | a | d | d | e | r | e |
| j | s | i | n | g | e | n | v | e | n |
| o | p | e | n | e | r | r | e | t | i |
| s | n | o | w | i | n | g | r | y | n |
| p | g | n | s | a | b | c | d | e | g |

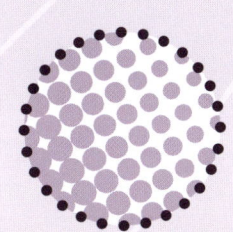

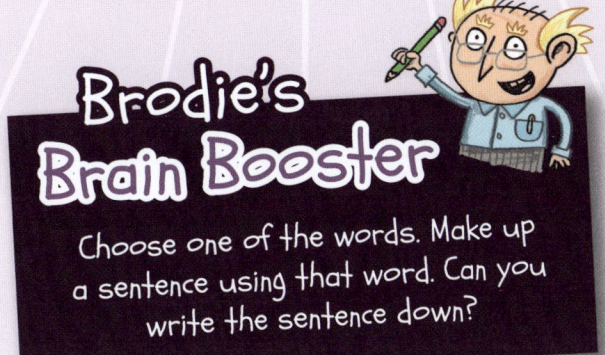

**Brodie's Brain Booster**

Choose one of the words. Make up a sentence using that word. Can you write the sentence down?

**Complete the chart.**
**Write the words with new endings.**

| Word | add **ing** | add **ed** | add **er** |
|---|---|---|---|
| play | | | |
| sing | | | |
| think | | | |
| start | | | |
| fly | | | |
| ring | | | |
| thank | | | |
| catch | | | |
| dress | | | |
| match | | | |

Brodie's
Brain Booster
Talk to an adult about why there
are gaps in the chart.

# Using exclamation marks

An exclamation mark goes at the end of an exclamation.

This is an exclamation mark.

**Start here** → Write the dot last

Write the exclamation mark carefully.

### Brodie's Brain Booster

Can you think of some exclamations?

Here are some exclamation sentences. Each one ends with an exclamation mark.

**What a big dog!**     **What a lovely day!**     **What a loud noise!**

Write some exclamations to go with these pictures.

_____

_____

# Little Red Riding Hood

What soft fur I have!

**Do you remember what Little Red Riding Hood said to the wolf when he was pretending to be her grandmother?**

**Write down Little Red Riding Hood's exclamations.**

_____

_____

_____

Brodie's Brain Booster

Do you think Little Red Riding Hood knew that it was the wolf?

# Puzzle pairs

I have black and white fur.

~~fish~~  jam  salt  pepper  nuts  tables  fork  bolts  socks

toast  bread  eggs  shoes  ham  butter  ~~chips~~  knife  chairs

**Which things go together? Find the pairs of words and join them with the word and. The first one has been done for you.**

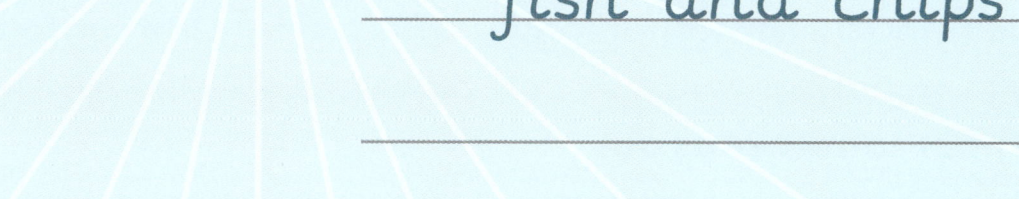

*fish and chips*

_____

_____

_____

_____

_____

_____

_____

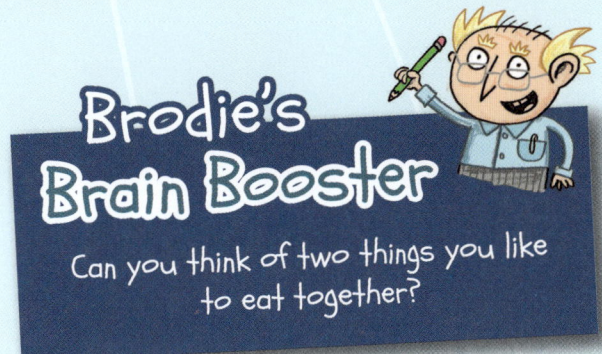

## Brodie's Brain Booster

Can you think of two things you like to eat together?

41

# Using and

I like running.      I like jumping.

**Two sentences.**

**We can use and to join the two sentences together.**

I like running and I like jumping.        **One sentence.**

**We can miss some words out.**

I like running and jumping.    ←    **One shorter sentence.**

**Write two sentences, one for each picture.**

_____

_____

**Join your sentences using and.**

_____

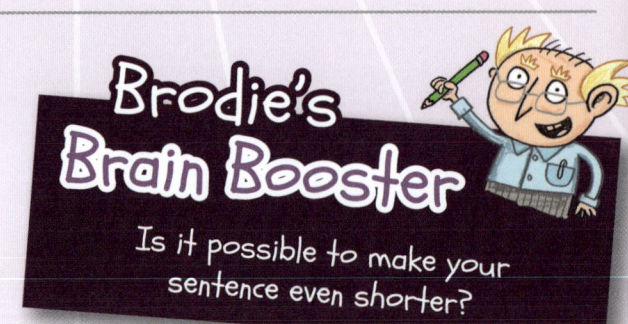
Brodie's
Brain Booster
Is it possible to make your
sentence even shorter?

# Using and again

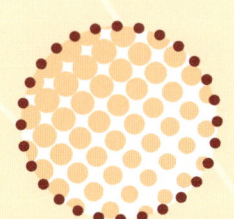

I got on the train.    I went to London.

I got up early **and** had my breakfast.

**Two sentences.**

We can use **and** to join the two sentences together.

I got on the train and I went to London.     **One sentence.**

We can miss some words out.

I got on the train and went to London.     **One shorter sentence.**

Here are two sentences, one for each picture.

_____

_____

Join your sentences using **and**.

_____

## Brodie's Brain Booster

Is it possible to make your sentence even shorter?

What a good dinner **and** what a nice sleep!

**What a lovely day!**　　**What a nice beach!**

**Two exclamation sentences.**

**We can join the two sentences together.**

**What a lovely day and what a nice beach!**　　**One exclamation sentence.**

**What a pretty cottage!**　　**What a beautiful view!**

**Join the sentences using and.**

_____

**Look at these two question sentences.**

**How old are you?**　　**What year are you in at school?**

**Join the question sentences using and.**

_____

Brodie's Brain Booster

Can you think of two more question sentences you could join together?

bat　　lemons　　hot　　cold　　ball　　bucket

saucer　　scarf　　spade　　hat　　oranges　　cup

**Find the pairs of words and join them with the word and.**

_____

_____

_____

_____

_____

_____

**Write an exclamation sentence about each dog. One has been done for you.**

*What a large dog!* _____

_____

_____

# ANSWERS

Use the answers to check your child's progress but also to give prompts and ideas if they are needed. Note that sometimes your child's answer may not match the answer given here but could be just as good!

 **p4**

kind mea**n**

ho**t** cold

ne**ar** f**ar**

e**a**sy h**ar**d

bi**g** little

### Brain Booster
Your child may suggest the word **down**.

**p5**

| Word | Opposite |
|------|----------|
| happy | unhappy |
| kind | unkind |
| afraid | unafraid |
| zip | unzip |
| block | unblock |
| cover | uncover |
| fit | unfit |
| hook | unhook |
| join | unjoin |
| lock | unlock |
| pack | unpack |
| tie | untie |
| safe | unsafe |

### Brain Booster
Your child may suggest the word untrue.

 **p6**

happy   merry   jolly   **unhappy**

**small**   big   huge   gigantic

kind   **unkind**   friendly   nice

**unpack**   load   fill   pack

thin   **thick**   narrow   small

afraid   scared   frightened   **unafraid**

hot   warm   **cold**   boiling

### Brain Booster
Your child may suggest the word **high**.

 **p7**

Your child may or may not use all of the words provided. These are the suggested sentences:

The boy has a cake. He is happy.

The girl has hurt her arm. She is unhappy.

### Brain Booster
Encourage your child to talk clearly about what makes her/him happy and to express this in a sentence.

 **p8**

Encourage your child to draw a picture and to write an appropriate sentence.

### Brain Booster
Talk about who makes your child happy: it could be a parent, grandparent, sibling or friend. Encourage her/him to compose an appropriate sentence.

 **p9**

Your child should compose at least two appropriate sentences. Remind them to start each one with a capital letter and to end it with a full stop. Example sentences: The dogs are chasing a cat. The cat is chasing the dogs now.

### Brain Booster
Discuss possible funny stories: do you have a pet who does funny things?

## Progress Test 1

How well does your child remember what they have practised? Note that some words may have more than one correct answer.

up down          wet dry
hot cold         tall short
sad happy        high low

able unable      unkind kind
zip unzip        unlock lock
wrap unwrap      unwise wise

uneven   unblock   **clean**   unsure

tall   **small**   big   huge

damp   soaking   wet   **dry**

Your child should write an appropriate sentence, e.g. The girl is happy.

**p11**

dog dogs          boy boys
girl girls        house houses
tree trees        car cars
table tables      chair chairs
clock clocks      book books
eye eyes          ear ears
nose noses        mouth mouths

### Brain Booster
mice

**p12**

potato potatoes       match matches
tomato tomatoes       bush bushes
church churches       echo echoes
ditch ditches         wish wishes
switch switches       kiss kisses
dish dishes           bus buses
splash splashes       hero heroes

### Brain Booster
children

**p13**

| a | b | t | a | b | l | e | s | c | d |
|---|---|---|---|---|---|---|---|---|---|
| e | f | g | h | o | i | j | k | l | d |
| m | n | o | c | o | w | s | p | q | i |
| r | s | t | u | k | v | o | w | x | s |
| b | o | x | e | s | y | c | z | a | h |
| b | c | d | e | f | g | k | h | i | e |
| j | k | s | p | l | a | s | h | e | s |
| l | m | n | o | p | q | r | s | t | u |
| v | w | x | t | r | e | e | s | y | z |
| p | i | n | s | a | b | c | d | e | f |

### Brain Booster
Your child should compose an appropriate sentence using one of the plural words.

## p14

| | |
|---|---|
| baby babies | mouse mice |
| child children | lady ladies |
| woman women | man men |

Example sentence: Here are two babies.

### Brain Booster
geese

## p15

flower plant **trees** shrub

car bus motorbike **lorries**

baby boy **children** girl

girls babies boys **child**

houses flat bungalow **house**

bricks tiles **brick** blocks

flower leaf petal **leaves**

### Brain Booster
deer

## p16

tooth teeth

goose geese

baby babies

deer deer

match matches

### Brain Booster
feet

## Progress Test 2

| | |
|---|---|
| girls girl | boys boy |
| matches match | foxes fox |
| dishes dish | rabbits rabbit |
| cars car buses bus | coaches coach |
| houses house | mice mouse |
| children child | ponies pony |
| ladies lady | men man |
| women woman | deer deer |
| teeth tooth | geese goose |
| lorries lorry | |

Your child should write three appropriate sentences.

## p18/p19

Your child should write appropriate sentences to tell the story. Examples: The cat wants to chase the birds. The birds are flying away. The birds are eating the cat food. The cat has seen them.

### Brain Booster
Discuss what happens next: Does the cat catch the birds?

## p20

Benjamin Connor Daisy Elliot Faith Gabriel Holly Isaac James Katie Letisha

### Brain Booster
Talk about all the children in your child's class.

## p21

Ali Blake Clara Dylan Eliza Felix Grace Harvey Isla Jude Katie Liam Muhammad Nur Omar Poppy Queenie Ruby Seth Tommy Umar Violet Willow Xavier Yara Zoe

### Brain Booster
Zara (or any other name beginning with Z)

## p22

Monday Tuesday Wednesday Thursday Friday Saturday Sunday

Friday Saturday Wednesday Sunday

### Brain Booster
Encourage your child to discuss their favourite day.

## p23

Your child should choose their favourite day and write about it.

### Brain Booster
Does your child know that Saturday and Sunday are at the weekend?

## Progress Test 3

Your child should write the names of four members of the family: parents, brothers, sisters, grandparents, aunts, uncles.

Monday Tuesday Wednesday Thursday Friday Saturday Sunday

Your child should write two sentences about the weekend.

## p25

Clockwise from top left:
Buckingham Palace
The Tower of London
Wembley Stadium
Tower Bridge

### Brain Booster
Discuss a visit to London. If your child hasn't been, where would she/he like to go in London?

## p26

Help your child to write your address.

### Brain Booster
Talk about the names of towns your child may know.

## p27

Your child should write appropriate sentences with capital letters used at the start and for any place names.

### Brain Booster
Talk about places your child likes.

## p28

Your child should answer the questions with facts they know.

### Brain Booster
Help your child to think of some questions.

## p29

Help your child to write some questions and to find answers to them.

### Brain Booster
Show your child an exclamation mark in their reading book.

## p30

Your child should answer the questions with facts they know.

### Brain Booster
Paris

## Progress Test 4

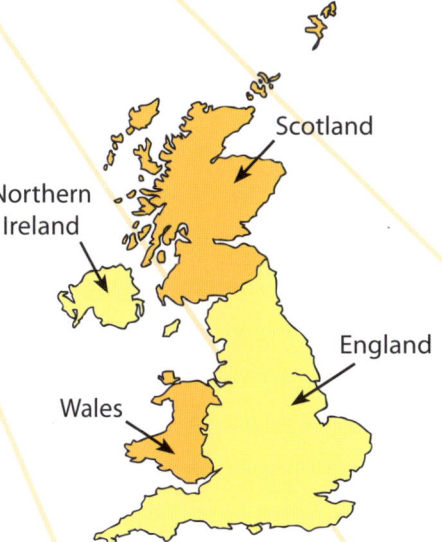

Your child should use an appropriate sentence and write a suitable question.

p32

playing jumping building parking singing acting drawing reading

Your child should write a sentence about one of the ing words. Check that there is a capital letter at the start and a full stop at the end.

**Brain Booster**
Talk about your child's favourite food.

p33

| a | b | t | a | b | l | e | s | c | d |
|---|---|---|---|---|---|---|---|---|---|
| e | f | g | h | a | s | k | i | n | g |
| m | c | o | c | r | w | s | n | q | a |
| r | r | t | u | k | v | o | g | x | r |
| b | o | x | e | i | y | c | i | a | d |
| b | s | d | e | n | g | k | n | i | e |
| j | s | i | n | g | i | n | g | e | n |
| l | i | n | o | p | q | r | s | t | i |
| s | n | o | w | i | n | g | s | y | n |
| p | g | n | s | a | b | c | d | e | g |

**Brain Booster**
Help your child to compose a suitable sentence.

p34

jumped looked barked played acted joined watched pecked

Your child should write a sentence about one of the ed words. Check that there is a capital letter at the start and a full stop at the end.

**Brain Booster**
Talk about a picture your child has painted.

p35

shout shouted

whisper whispered

bark barked

roar roared

yell yelled

**Brain Booster**
Other sound words include: laugh laughed bang banged crash crashed growl growled

p36

jumper dancer quicker fresher hunter buzzer sender singer

Your child should write a sentence about one of the er words. Check that there is a capital letter at the start and a full stop at the end.

**Brain Booster**
Talk about your child's hobby or interest: can she/he use a word that ends in er?

p37

| a | b | w | a | t | c | h | e | r | d |
|---|---|---|---|---|---|---|---|---|---|
| e | f | a | h | a | s | k | i | i | g |
| m | i | l | l | e | r | s | n | n | a |
| r | r | k | u | k | e | o | g | g | r |
| b | o | e | e | i | a | c | i | e | d |
| b | s | r | e | a | d | d | e | r | e |
| j | s | i | n | g | e | n | v | e | n |
| o | p | e | n | e | r | r | e | t | i |
| s | n | o | w | i | n | g | r | y | n |
| p | g | n | s | a | b | c | d | e | g |

**Brain Booster**
Help your child to compose a suitable sentence.

## Progress Test 5

| Word | add ing | add ed | add er |
|---|---|---|---|
| play | playing | played | player |
| sing | singing | ✕ | singer |
| think | thinking | ✕ | thinker |
| start | starting | started | starter |
| fly | flying | ✕ | flyer |
| ring | ringing | ✕ | ringer |
| thank | thanking | thanked | ✕ |
| catch | catching | ✕ | catcher |
| dress | dressing | dressed | dresser |
| match | matching | matched | ✕ |

There are gaps in the chart because some words don't exist: eg instead of 'singed' we say 'sang'

p39

What a long worm! What a fierce cat!

**Brain Booster**
Help your child to think of other exclamations.

p40

What big eyes you have! What big ears you have! What big teeth you have!

**Brain Booster**
What does your child think about this part of the story?

p41

fish and chips bread and butter ham and eggs toast and jam salt and pepper shoes and socks knife and fork table and chairs nuts and bolts

**Brain Booster**
What does your child like to eat?

p42

The girl likes playing tennis. She likes swimming.

The girl likes playing tennis and she likes swimming.

**Brain Booster**
The girl likes tennis and swimming.

p43

We packed the car and we went to the beach.

**Brain Booster**
We packed the car and went to the beach.

p44

What a pretty cottage and what a beautiful view!

How old are you and what year are you in at school?

**Brain Booster**

Help your child to think of some questions.

## Progress Test 6

bat and ball bucket and spade hot and cold oranges and lemons hat and scarf cup and saucer

Example sentences: What a tiny dog! What a huge dog!